PAINTING & DECORATING FRAMES

PHILLIP C. MYER

NORTH LIGHT BOOKS
CINCINNATI, OHIO

A NOTE ABOUT SAFETY

Due to toxicity concerns, most art and craft material manufacturers have begun labeling their products with proper health warnings or nontoxic seals. It is always important to read a manufacturer's label when using a product for the first time. Follow any warnings about not using the product when pregnant or contemplating pregnancy, about keeping the product out of reach of children or about incompatible products. Always work in a well-ventilated room when using products with fumes.

The information in this book is presented in good faith, but no warranty is given, nor results guaranteed, nor is freedom from any patent to be inferred. Since we have no control over physical conditions surrounding the application of products, techniques and information herein, the publisher and author disclaim any liability for results.

Painting & Decorating Frames. Copyright © 1998 by Phillip C. Myer. Manufactured in Singapore. All rights reserved. No part of this book may be reproduced in any form or by any electronic or mechanical means including information storage and retrieval systems without permission in writing from the publisher, except by a reviewer, who may quote brief passages in a review. Published by North Light Books, an imprint of F&W Publications, Inc., 1507 Dana Avenue, Cincinnati, Ohio 45207. (800) 289-0963. First edition.

Other fine North Light Books are available from your local bookstore, art supply store or direct from the publisher.

02 01 00 99 98   5 4 3 2 1

Library of Congress Cataloging-in-Publication Data

Myer, Phillip C.
    Painting & decorating frames / Phillip C. Myer.
        p.   cm. — (Creative finishes series)
    Includes index.
    ISBN 0-89134-803-4 (alk. paper)
    1. Painting.   2. Decoration and ornament.   3. Wood finishing.   4. Picture frames and framing.   5. Handicraft.
    I. Title.   II. Series.
TT385.M944   1998
749'.7—dc21   97-53121
                                                    CIP

Edited by Jennifer King
Production Edited by Michelle Kramer
Cover designed by Mary Barnes Clark

Dedication

I would like to dedicate this book to my niece,
Whitney Amanda Williams,
whose zest for life is very motivating
for my creative inspirations.

SPECIAL THANKS

Thanks and gratitude go to the individuals who have assisted with this book. Many thanks to the manufacturers and their representatives that I have had the pleasure of working with: Dee Silver of Silver Brush Limited (Golden Natural and faux brush lines), Margo Christensen of Martin/F. Weber Company (Prima Artist's Acrylics) and John McDonald of Back Street, Inc. (Faux Easy glazes). I would also like to thank the manufacturers and representatives who produce ready-to-decorate picture frames for artists and crafters: Dean Benamy of House Works Ltd., Cindy Perrin-Gorden of Walnut Hollow and Kathy Jorgensen of HY-JO MFG Imports Corp.

ABOUT THE AUTHOR

Phillip C. Myer has been painting for over twenty-five years. He is the author of *Creative Paint Finishes for the Home*, *Creative Paint Finishes for Furniture*, *Painting & Decorating Boxes*, *Painting & Decorating Tables* and *Painting & Decorating Cabinets & Chests* (North Light Books), as well as twelve softcover books on tole and decorative painting. He has appeared on how-to decorating television segments on *Decorating With Style*, *Home Matters* and *Handmade by Design*. Myer has also produced four instructional videos on decorating techniques. A member of the Society of Decorative Painters for over twenty-two years, Myer teaches seminars across the United States, Canada and Argentina, and at his Atlanta-based studios. Myer and his business partner, Andy Jones, create custom-painted furniture and interior decorating through their business—PCM Studios.

TABLE OF CONTENTS

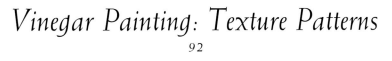

INTRODUCTION

*D*ecorating picture frames may not have occurred to you before viewing this book, probably because there is a wide variety of ready-made and decorated picture frames on the market. These ready-made frames will often fit your decorating needs in your home. But when it comes to customizing your home to make it uniquely personal, you'll want to create a few one-of-a-kind picture frames. Picture frames house some of your most cherished memories—from family photographs and special memorabilia to certificates and awards. Why not make the frame special, too!

The techniques taught in this book range from simple, understated effects to those with vibrancy and great interest. When choosing a technique, remember the basic rule of picture framing and matting: Don't let the frame or mat treatment become so busy that it overpowers what's inside the frame. This approach is definitely to be followed when framing serious artwork or photography. For more casual photos or mementos, though, I think it is acceptable to decorate the frame surface in a more playful, patterned, busy style.

The projects in this book are to be used as sources of inspiration. Start with unfinished frames, standard finished frames or old flea market or tag sale frames. Then you can easily coordinate your picture frame decorating with your home by choosing colors from your fabrics, wall covering or rugs. Just change the color scheme or patterning shown in these demonstrations to match your needs; for example, you can repeat a design motif from an upholstery fabric on your frame for a further decorating tie-in. Good luck and enjoy decorating frames. 🌿

Phillip C. Myer

BEFORE YOU BEGIN

*Y*ou'll need to gather an assortment of tools and materials to decorate the frames in this book. These basic supplies will give you a "creative toolbox" to use on future projects.

GETTING STARTED

There are a few things to familiarize yourself with before beginning to decorate frames. Knowledge and organization are the keys to successful results when executing the techniques taught in this book. Take the time to read the next few pages thoroughly to review the general tools, basic techniques, and transfer, preparation, trimming and finishing methods. Although each project in this book is a self-contained unit featuring the necessary supplies and step-by-step illustrations and instructions, the following "foundation" material will get you started on the right road.

PAINTS AND GLAZES

The house paint, art material and craft supply industries have begun developing and manufacturing environmentally friendly, water-based products. These products are nontoxic, have little to no odor and clean up easily with soap and water. The projects in this book are executed with a majority of these new-age, environmentally protective products.

Acrylic Paints

To create your own color mixtures in small quantities appropriate for painting frames, a set of artist's grade or student grade acrylic paints in true artist's pigments will prove useful. I like working with Prima Acrylics in the following colors, which provide a good, basic palette for making any color combination: Alizarin Crimson, Bright Red, Burnt Sienna, Burnt Umber, Cadmium Orange, Cadmium Red Light, Cadmium Yellow Light, Iridescent Gold, Iridescent White, Mars Black, Metallic Gold, Phthalo Green, Raw Umber, Titanium White and Ultramarine Blue.

Latex-Based Paints

You'll need to have a selection of base paints (base coats) to function as the foundation for the paint and craft techniques. Following instructions for each technique, you'll use either a flat or semigloss latex-based paint. You can have these colors mixed at a hardware store or home improvement center. Today, most house paint departments offer computer color matching to match any reference material you bring them (fabric, wallpaper or carpet). For the frame projects in this book, a quart of base paint will provide you with more than enough paint. If you would like to purchase a smaller quantity of base paint, look for 2-, 8- or 16-ounce (59, 236 or 472ml) squeeze bottles of acrylics at art and craft stores. You won't be able to receive custom color matches with these ready-made paints, but you'll pay less and waste less.

Acrylic Glazing Medium

Many of the frame projects require the use of a colored glaze to create the technique. You can create this colored glaze mixture by adding artist's acrylic or latex house paints to a clear glazing medium. There are many ready-made clear glazing products on the market, or you can create your own. To make your own clear, acrylic glazing medium, mix equal amounts of water-based polyurethane varnish, acrylic retarder, and water in a jar and stir thoroughly.

Whichever type of clear glazing medium you choose, you'll want a glaze product that has a sufficient open time (working time) for manipulating the wet glaze and paint in the desired technique. Due to the size of most frame projects, you'll require at least ten to fifteen minutes of open time to achieve successful results.

Ready-Made Colored Glazes

Ready-made pretinted glazes require no mixing or measuring and are ready to use from the jar. I've used Anita's Faux Easy glazes for many of the colored glazes found in this book. There are twenty-four colors in the Faux Easy glaze collection, and these colors can be intermixed to create new custom colors. Standard Faux Easy

colors include Black, Brown Bark, Burgundy, Butter Cream, Copper, Cranberry, Dark Brown, Dark Williamsburg, Forest Green, Gold, Indian Brown, Midnight Blue, Moss Green, Old Gold, Peacock, Poppy Red, Pumpkin, Rose Petal, Silver, Sunshine, Verdigris, Washed Denim, White and Wine.

MATERIALS
Decoupage Glue and Craft Glue

To complete the gluing steps found in several techniques, decoupage glue and craft glue will be required. White craft glue, which is extremely thick, will not work for decoupage paper adhesion methods. However, you can make decoupage glue by taking a white craft glue that is somewhat fluid and thinning it with additional water until it reaches a flowing consistency.

Water-Based Varnishes

Water-based polyurethane varnishes are used throughout the techniques in this book. These varnishes, such as Anita's, provide durability, a broad open time, and water- and alcohol-resistance, more so than standard acrylic water-based varnishes. As you finish the frames with different techniques, you can choose a satin, semigloss or gloss varnish to add variety to your work.

Spray Finishes

Today, there are several types of environment-friendly spray finishes. You can choose clear or colored acrylic-based sprays—in satin, semigloss or gloss sheens—to coat, seal and protect your decorated frames.

BRUSHES

As you build your technique repertoire, you can also build your brush collection. There are several brushes that are considered "workhorse" brushes and are listed in the supplies of just about every technique. These brushes will get used over and over but, if taken care of, will last a long time. All brushes listed here are produced by Silver Brush Limited.

Base Coat Bristle Brush

This is a 3-inch brush made of natural hairs cut at a tapered angle to form a sharp, chisel edge. This edge allows you to paint a straight line, control base paint application, work the brush into tight spots and stroke on a smooth, even base coat.

Glaze Brush

The glaze brush is 1 inch (2.5cm) wide, also made from soft, natural hairs cut at a tapered angle. The natural hairs soak in a sufficient amount of glaze and allow you to stroke a fair amount of it on the surface. Synthetic hair brushes do not provide this control because the artificial hair cannot drink in moisture.

Varnish Brush

A 1-inch brush made of natural hair allows you great control when applying a water-based varnish. The hairs drink in the varnish then release it when you apply pressure to the brush. This size brush also lets you get varnish into tight, recessed areas.

Silver Mop Brush

The mop brush in a ¾-inch (1.9cm) size, made of soft, natural hairs, allows you to move the paint and blend with great ease. The small shape enables you to get into specific areas to control the blending techniques.

Golden Natural Flats

Flat brushes in nos. 8, 12 and 16 provide a range of sizes to complete detail work. These brushes are made from a combination of natural and synthetic hairs. They have sharp chisel edges to access specific areas and to paint clean, sharp edges or lines on a surface.

Golden Natural Round

A no. 4 round brush provides a fine point for detail and cleanup. Made of natural and synthetic hairs, it will hold a good deal of paint.

Golden Natural Script Liner

A no. 1 script liner will provide crisp line work. This brush's hairs are about ½ to ¾ inch (1cm to 2cm) longer than a standard liner brush's hairs, so they hold more paint and create a longer detail line.

Sponge Brushes

Polyfoam brushes (sponge brushes) in 1- or 2-inch (2.5cm or 5.1cm) sizes are ideal for trim and some base coat painting. They can also be used to apply glue. Do not use them for varnish application, though; a natural hair varnish brush provides better results.

TOOLS

The following tools are used in various techniques throughout this book. Refer to the supply list found with each technique to determine what you need for a specific project.

Tracing Paper

Transparent tracing paper in 12" × 16" (30cm × 41cm) pads or in rolls 24 inches (61cm) long will be used for tracing and drawing pattern designs.

Palette Knife and Paint Stirrers

A palette knife with a long, wide, flexible blade is required to thoroughly mix the paint and glaze mixtures. Wood paint stirrers are needed to mix quarts of paint.

Wax-Coated Palette and Foam Plates

A 12" × 16" (30cm × 41cm) wax-coated palette and flat foam plates (with no divided sections) can be used as surfaces for mixing small amounts of acrylic/latex paint and acrylic color glaze.

Metal Rulers

Rulers in 12- and 36-inch (30 and 91cm) lengths with corked backings raising the rulers above the edge of your work surface will be used for measuring and ruling pen work.

Ruling Pen

A ruling pen can be filled with thin-consistency paint to draw a fine trim or detail line. It has a slot area for holding paint and a turn screw to adjust the line width.

Craft Knife (X-Acto No. 11)

A craft knife with a sharp blade is ideal for cutting and scoring surfaces.

Brayer

A rubber brayer will roll over a surface and apply pressure to smooth out an area. It's handy for laying down decoupage prints and sections of paper.

Credit Card

The hard plastic edge of a credit card can be used as a burnishing tool for rubbing down the edge of tape when masking an area or for securing foil in place. The tip of a large metal spoon will provide similar results.

Tapes

Several types of tapes are required when painting. They should all be repositionable so you can remove the tape without harming the coating below. The white Safe Release tape and blue Long-Mask tape manufactured by 3M provide good edges for painting straight lines. Easy Mask's brown painter's tape has an adhesive on half of one side of the tape for broader coverage and protection.

Sandpaper

A variety of sandpaper in coarse (#60), medium (#100), fine (#150) and ultrafine (#400 and #600) grades will be required to smooth out or distress surfaces.

Miscellaneous Items

The following items are some standard household and painting workshop tools. Many are considered tools "that go without mentioning" when referring to basic methods used in this book. For example, if you are using a quart of paint, you'll need something to open it with—a paint key.

- Acetone
- Acrylic retarder
- Bar soap
- Cheesecloth
- Clear acrylic spray
- Containers—small and large margarine tubs
- Cotton rags
- Drop cloths
- Dry ballpoint pen or stylus
- Erasers
- Gray graphite paper
- Hammer
- Murphy's Oil Soap
- Paint key
- Paper sacks
- Paste wax
- Pencils
- Plastic gloves
- Putty knife
- Sanding block
- Spackling compound
- Steel wool—#0000
- Tack cloth
- Toothbrush
- White transfer paper
- Wood putty

BASICS

*T*here are a few basic techniques that apply to most of these frame decorating projects. That's why it is a good idea to read the following information to prepare yourself for the painting adventures that lie ahead. 🙢

PRIMING AND PREPARING

The frames that have been decorated with paint or covered with paper require a coat of primer to seal surfaces and create a "tooth" for good adhesion. A white, stain-blocking primer,

such as KILZ 2, provides a solid foundation on wood and papier maché surfaces. Apply one or two coats, lightly sanding when dry.

BASE COATING

An important step in the process of decorating a frame is applying a base paint to the surface. It is critical for this foundation color to go on

smoothly. To achieve smooth, even base coat coverage, you should follow a few easy tips: Always load the base coat bristle brush with plenty of paint, saturating the bristles with color, then lightly stroke the bristles across the side of the paint container. You only need to load the brush one to two inches (2.5cm to 5.1cm) from the chisel edge. Next, stroke color on the surface. Tackle one section of the frame at a time. Apply paint into all recessed trim areas first, then proceed to the larger, flat areas. Always stroke in long, fluid strokes; short, choppy strokes make for a messy-looking

base coat and can be magnified when decorative treatments are placed over them. Apply one coat and let it dry thoroughly, following the drying schedule found on the paint label. If you do not allow proper curing (drying) time, the next coat can sag and cause curtaining. Lightly sand between coats with a piece of paper sack or fine sandpaper. Remove dust with a tack cloth and proceed with base coating.

CLEANING BRUSHES

Once you have invested in good-quality brushes, it is important to take care of them. When you are not going to use a brush for a period of time and it has paint and glaze in it, you should stop and clean it. Water-based products dry fairly rapidly even when mixed with retarders. So when you finish painting a section, place your brush in a container of water. When finished for the day, take your brushes to the sink and wash them thoroughly with Murphy's Oil Soap and water. Rinse the brush and wash a second time to verify that all traces of color have been removed from the brush's hairs. The hairs of the brush extend past the metal ferrule at the base of the bristles, and you want to remove any paint that may be residing there. Shake off excess moisture and allow the brushes to dry thoroughly before storing.

If you've allowed acrylic to dry in the brush's hairs, a small amount of acetone will work some or all of the dried acrylic out of the hairs. However, the acetone may be harmful and harsh to certain types of brush hairs.

TRACING AND TRANSFERRING

Some of the frame projects require the use of a pattern. To use the pat-

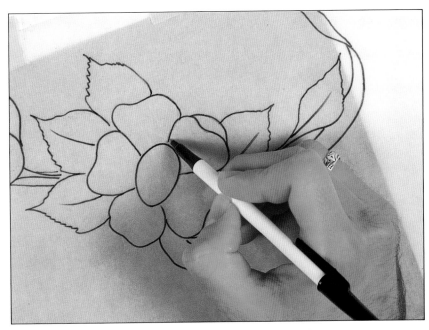

terns given in the back of this book or to pick up designs elsewhere, you'll need to first carefully trace the design's basic outline by covering it with tracing paper and going over the lines with a pencil or fine marker.

To transfer the pattern onto the frame, tape the traced design in place with several pieces of tape. Depending on the background color, you'll slip either gray graphite paper (for light backgrounds) or white transfer

paper (for dark backgrounds) under the traced design and go over the basic outline with a dried-out ballpoint pen or stylus. Lift the tracing paper from time to time to see how well the design is transferring.

TRIMMING WITH RULING PEN

A ruling pen can add a fine line of color to a frame's surface. Start by thinning the desired acrylic color

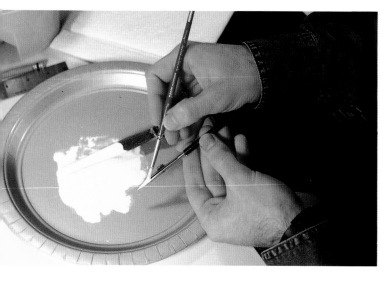

with plenty of water. The paint mixture should be quite fluid but still have a little body to it. Next, load a round brush with thinned paint and stroke alongside the ruling pen's open slot to deposit the paint in the pen. Be sure to wipe away excess paint on the sides of the pen. Then, using a cork-backed, raised ruler (so the paint does not seep under), hold the pen at a 45° angle and stroke alongside the ruler at a steady pace, allowing the paint to flow out in an even line. Complete all parallel lines first, let them dry and then add perpendicular lines.

FINISHING

After you've decorated the frame, you want to protect it. Use a natural-hair varnish brush to apply at least two coats of a water-based polyurethane varnish over the surface. Always be on the lookout for any varnish runs. Allow each coat to dry thoroughly before applying another coat.

For an elaborate, glasslike finish, you can apply a series of three coats of varnish, rub with #0000 steel wool, apply three more coats of varnish, rub with steel wool, apply three more coats, rub with steel wool and apply the last coat of varnish.

BACKING

After you have inserted the items you wish to house in your decorated frame and decided whether to include glass, you'll need to finish the back of the frame and apply a proper hanger. Proper backing completes your framing project.

A simple brown paper or paper with a simple pattern will finish your project with a professional look. Cut the paper about one inch larger than the frame's perimeter using a ruler and a craft knife. Then place double-stick tape or thin-consistency glue on all four edges of the back of the frame. Adhere the paper to the tape or glue. If using glue, clean up any excess on the side of the frame with a sponge.

Let dry. Then cut the excess paper around the perimeter with a knife.

To attach hanging hardware, insert two screw eyes about one quarter of the way down from the top edge on the right and left sides on the frame. Screw in place. Loop picture-framing wire through both screw eyes and secure in place by twisting and wrapping over the excess wire. Place two small felt pads on the bottom corners of the frame to bring the frame out level from the wall.

As a finishing touch, personalize the back of the frame with your signature or business card.

COLOR CHOICES

The starting point for decorating a picture frame is choosing the technique you want to execute. Once that decision is made, you'll need to work out a color direction. Remember that simply changing the colors will dramatically alter the finished look of the technique.

In the three examples, the same technique was executed—gilding and distressing (found on pages 21-25)—but a different color palette was chosen for each frame. The frame for the infant's photo has been base coated in a bright red and gilded with silver leaf. These two distinct colors and their divergent values create strong contrast. The frame with the photo of the small child has been base coated in leaf green and gilded in copper leaf. These two colors are distinct but their values are closer so there is less contrast. In the last example, with the photo of the sailor, the frame's base coat is gold and the gilding is in gold leaf so the contrast is subtle. By simply working with the juxtaposition of colors and their values, you can create an endless rainbow of creative solutions to your decorating efforts.

If you are new to working with colors, experiment with sample boards or scrap trim moldings. Try a variety of color combinations or rely on reference materials found in your home—wallpaper, fabric or rug coloration. Don't be afraid of color; it can become your best decorating friend.

FRAMING IDEAS

There are many items you can insert into just about any decorated frame. Here are a few ideas to get you started.

Bulletin Board

By inserting a tight cork surface into a frame, you can customize an attractive bulletin board for a home office, child's bedroom or kitchen phone area. It's a great way to create a message center in a busy home.

Mirror

Carefully measure your decorated frame. Then go to a frame shop, glass and mirror shop or hardware store and have a piece of mirror cut to size. Insert the mirror into your decorated frame, and place it by the front or back door, in a small powder room or anywhere you wish to have that last minute review of hair and makeup before leaving the house.

Certificate

When you or others are honored through achievements, you should frame these certificates or diplomas for posterity.

Child's Art

A decorated frame with no permanent backing can act as a revolving and ever changing art display. Make it simple to pop out the child's drawing and insert the new masterpiece so you can bring attention to the bud-

ding artist's work. Use large, bendable metal points and a thick piece of cardboard behind the artwork. Don't bother with glass.

Memorabilia

Place various mementos from a special occasion in one frame. For example, place flowers, invitation, photos and matchbook from a wedding, anniversary or special party.

Family Photo

Insert old family photos on acid-free board with acid-free, archival photo corners, and place spacers so glass does not come in contact with the photo. For special archival items, see your local framer for advice and assistance on preserving these cherished items.

PAPER COVERING: MARBLEIZED

Photo of detail on marbleized paper covering.

*M*arbleized papers are used often in frame and mat decorating techniques. For example, a French style of matting uses the marbleized papers in thin strips alongside a fine colored line. On these projects, the French style of mat decoration was applied to wide frames. Sections of the frames have been trimmed with patterned papers, allowing the coordinated base coat color to show through in some areas. The fine line work gives the frame a flair of elegance. 🙾

PAPER COVERING: MARBLEIZED

TOOLS AND MATERIALS

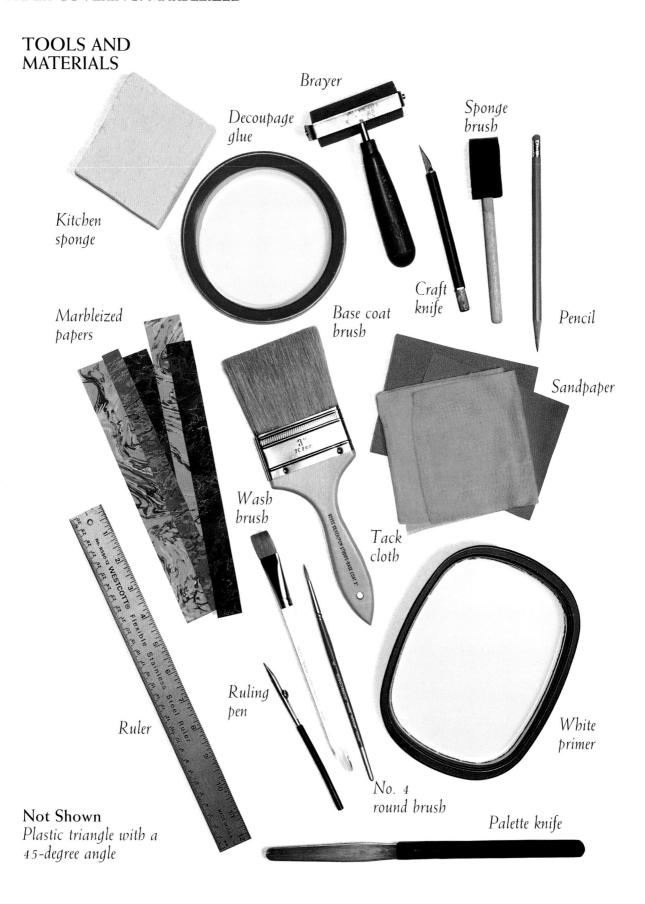

Kitchen sponge

Decoupage glue

Brayer

Sponge brush

Craft knife

Pencil

Marbleized papers

Base coat brush

Sandpaper

Wash brush

Tack cloth

Ruler

Ruling pen

No. 4 round brush

White primer

Not Shown
Plastic triangle with a 45-degree angle

Palette knife

COLOR CHIPS—LATEX SEMIGLOSS PAINT

Metallic Gold
Golden Ochre
Forest Green

1 Using the base coat brush, prime the frame with white primer. Let dry. After the primer has dried, sand the surface and remove the sanding dust with a tack cloth. Coat the frame in a coordinating color found in the marbleized paper. In these examples, the base coat colors of Metallic Gold and Golden Ochre highlight the lighter tones found in the papers.

PAPER COVERING: MARBLEIZED

2 Determine how wide you wish to make the strips of marbleized papers and where you wish to place the strips and colored lines within the width of the frame. Lightly mark the proper placements on the picture frame and the correct measurements on the back of the papers using a pencil and ruler. Use a craft knife to cut out the paper strips, using the ruler as a guide. Use a plastic triangle to cut the ends at 45-degree angles. Leave a slight amount of extra paper on the angled ends so the mitered corners overlap.

3 Using a wash brush, apply a smooth coating of decoupage glue on the back of the paper. Quickly place the piece of paper on the frame following your pencil guidelines. Smooth the paper with a brayer and lightly rub with a slightly moist sponge.

4 Let the first layer of paper strips dry before adding a second, overlapping layer. If desired, cut away sections of the second strip of paper to create a design motif. Here a corner and center cutaway were created. Place glue on the back of the additional paper strips and apply firm pressure with the brayer to achieve good adhesion between the different layers of papers.

5 Remove all traces of glue by wiping the surface with a damp sponge. To add fine line work, use a palette knife to thin the acrylic paint with water until it reaches a fluid consistency. Load the ruling pen with paint using a round brush. Run the pen along the edge of the ruler to deposit a fine line of color next to the paper strips.

GILDING: DISTRESSED

Photo of detail on gilded, distressed frame.

*G*ilded finishes are the most popular decorating techniques for frames. The glimmering and shiny qualities of gilding are unmatched in any other method. Metallic paints can come close to resembling a gilded surface, but when the two are compared side by side, there really isn't a resemblance. In these examples, the gilding has been completed following standard methods and then aged through a distressing technique. You can gild a frame in a variety of metal leaves—from the traditional gold leaf and silver leaf to copper leaf and variegated leaf. ?ই

GILDING: DISTRESSED

TOOLS AND MATERIALS

Metal leaf—
book of 5½″ × 5½″
(14cm × 14cm) sheets

Cardboard box

Wax-coated
freezer paper

Paste wax

Sandpaper

Tack cloth

Leaf sizing—
oil base

Soft natural-hair
brush

Sponge
brush

Base coat
brush

White primer

Scissors

Steel wool—#0000

Mineral spirits

Cotton rag

COLOR CHIPS—LATEX SEMIGLOSS PAINT

Red Oxide
Metallic Gold
Black

Bright Red
Leaf Green
Burnt Brown

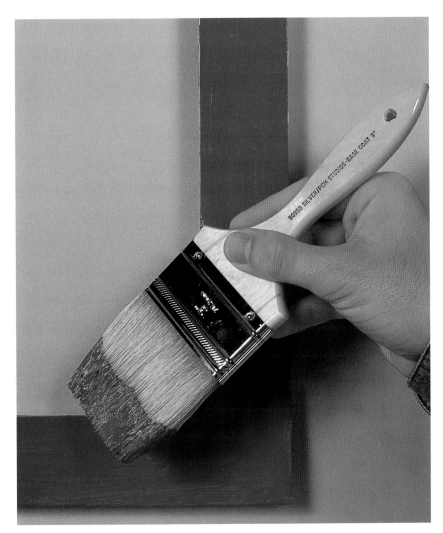

1 Using the base coat brush, prime the frame with white primer. Let dry. Sand and remove the sanding dust with a tack cloth. Apply the desired base color to the frame. For gold leaf use either Red Oxide (bold contrast) or Metallic Gold (subtle contrast); for silver leaf use either Bright Red (bold contrast) or Black (subtle contrast); for copper leaf use either Leaf Green (bold contrast) or Burnt Brown (subtle contrast). Apply several coats for an opaque coverage.

2 Apply an even coverage of leaf sizing with a sponge brush. Let the sizing reach its working state (tacky quality) by following the timing guidelines found on the product's label. While you're waiting, cut metal leaf sheets into appropriate sizes for the width and height of each side of the frame. (Remove tissue between leaf sheets one at a time.) Cut the freezer paper into sheets slightly larger than the cut leaves, and rub the wax side of the paper over the leaf sheets. This will cause the leaf to temporarily adhere to the freezer paper. Place the leaf/freezer paper over the sticky sizing on the frame. Rub the leaf lightly in place. Repeat this process, overlapping each sheet until the frame is covered with leaf.

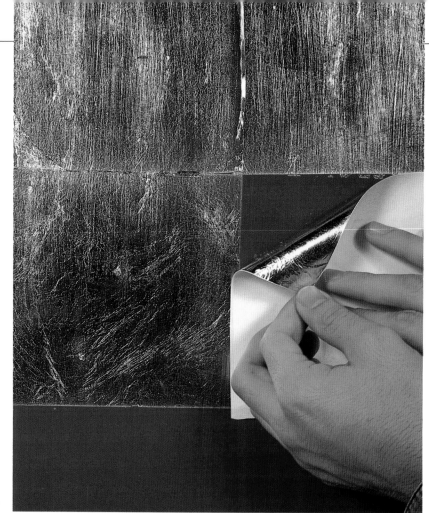

3 Let the leaf sheets and sizing dry overnight. You can remove any overlapping flaps of leaf by burnishing the surface. To do this, pick up a soft natural-hair brush and stroke gently across the flaps. Brush these extra leaf pieces (called skewings) into a box to save for another project.

4 Buff the surface lightly with a clean cotton rag to remove any small fringes of leaf you've missed. Don't handle the leafed areas with your hands, because the oils from your skin can leave marks. To distress the gilded surface, load a piece of fine steel wool with a small amount of paste wax and begin rubbing the frame.

5 Continue rubbing the frame surface with the steel wool until you have rubbed through the gilding and exposed the base coat color below. You can remove as little or as much of the gilding as you desire. Be sure to rub with the grain (natural direction) of each section of the frame, enough to remove any high spots in the structure of the frame.

TEXTURIZING: CHEESECLOTH

Photo of detail on cheesecloth texture.

*W*hen adhered to a picture frame, the wide weave of cheesecloth contributes a rich, tactile quality. The dimensional pattern provides many recessed areas which can collect color and glazes, adding even more interest when painted. Or the cheesecloth can be painted a solid color to provide a simpler, tone-on-tone look, enhanced by the shadows cast by the cheesecloth's texture. Other lightweight, textured fabrics, such as thin gauze, can be used for this technique, too. ❧

TOOLS AND MATERIALS

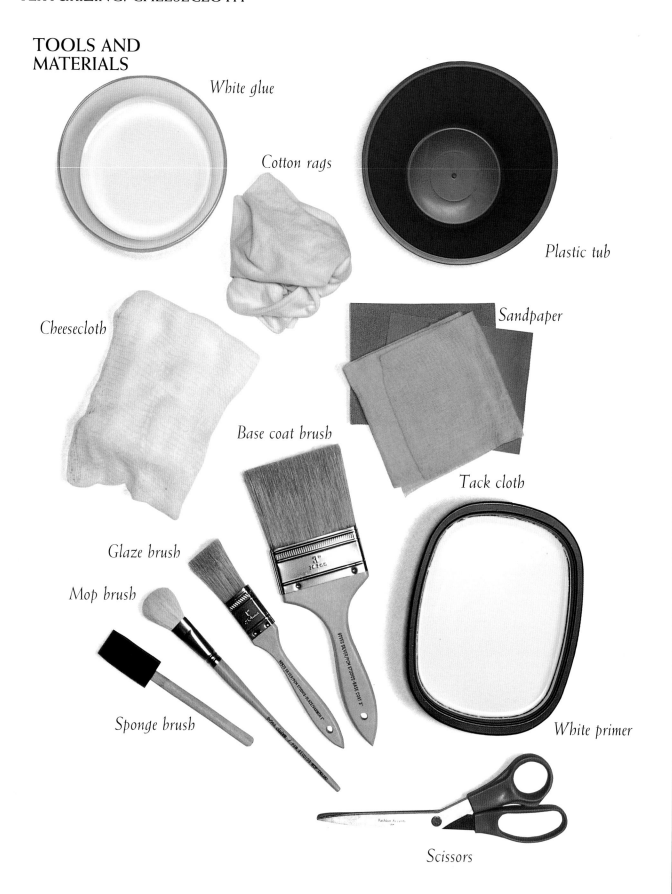

White glue

Cotton rags

Plastic tub

Cheesecloth

Sandpaper

Base coat brush

Tack cloth

Glaze brush

Mop brush

Sponge brush

White primer

Scissors

COLOR CHIPS—LATEX SEMIGLOSS PAINT, WATER-BASED GLAZE

Ecru latex
Dark Brown glaze
Indian Brown glaze

1 Using the base coat brush, prime the frame with white primer. Let dry, then sand lightly with a fine grade of sandpaper. Remove any sanding dust with a tack cloth.

TEXTURIZING: CHEESECLOTH

2 Thin the white craft glue slightly with water in a small plastic tub. Brush a liberal amount of thin, creamy glue on the frame's surface with a sponge brush. Cut a sheet of cheesecloth slightly larger than the perimeter of the frame. Embed the cheesecloth in the glue, and place it over the front of the frame. Pull the excess cheesecloth around the sides of the frame to the back. Next cut an opening in the cheesecloth in the center of the frame, leaving about ½ inch (1cm) of fabric (depending on the width of the frame) extending beyond the frame's inside edges, toward the center of the frame. Remove the center portion of the cheesecloth. Cut diagonal lines in the inside corners and wrap the excess cheesecloth to the back of the frame.

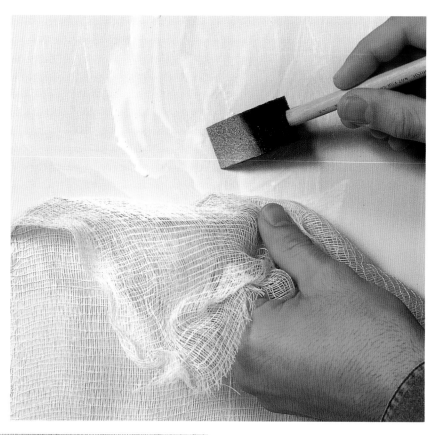

3 Once the glue is dry, base coat the cheesecloth. A light cream-colored semigloss latex paint was used in this example. Apply several coats until an opaque coverage is achieved. Let dry.

4 Load the glaze application brush with Dark Brown water-based glaze and begin brushing and scrubbing this color into the texture. Place random patches of this color over the frame surface. Wipe brush and then pick up Indian Brown glaze to place additional color patches until the entire frame is covered with alternating shades of brown.

5 After coating the frame with the glaze colors, use a cotton rag to remove the excess glaze by wiping in a circular motion. Soften any areas of the glaze by dusting the surface with a mop brush. Let glaze dry twenty-four hours.

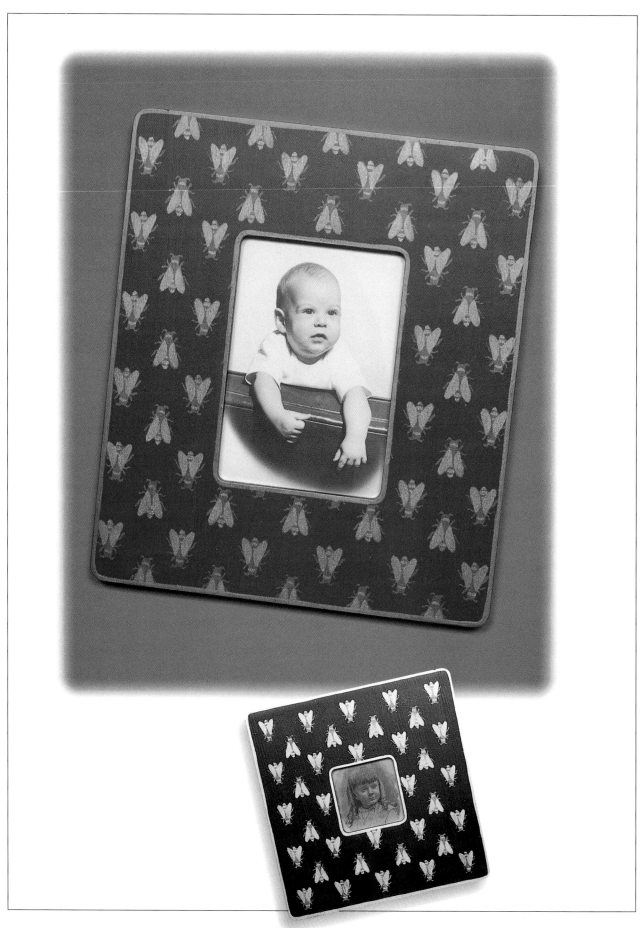

STENCILLING: BEE MOTIF

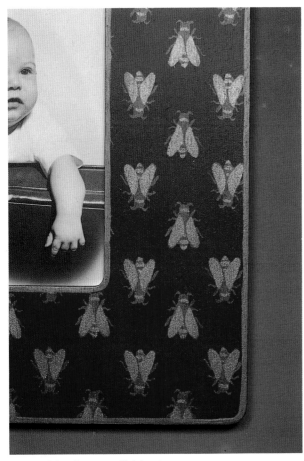

Photo of detail on stencilled bee frame.

*S*tencilling techniques and a charming bee motif can add up to a classic look. In these examples, metallic paint was used to provide the sophistication of expensive wallpaper. Of course, a grid of bees in a medium value could also be stencilled over a lighter base coat color to create a subtle, tone-on-tone effect. For a more casual look, you could stencil the bees in a random pattern as if they are flying around the surface of the frame. ❧

TOOLS AND MATERIALS

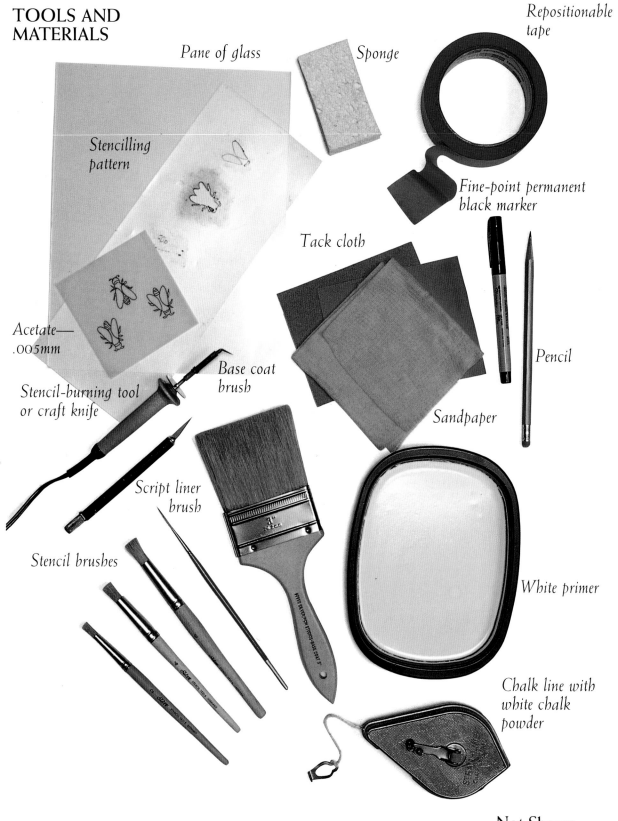

Repositionable tape

Pane of glass

Sponge

Stencilling pattern

Fine-point permanent black marker

Tack cloth

Acetate—.005mm

Pencil

Stencil-burning tool or craft knife

Base coat brush

Sandpaper

Script liner brush

Stencil brushes

White primer

Chalk line with white chalk powder

Not Shown
Ruler

COLOR CHIPS—LATEX FLAT PAINT, ACRYLIC PAINT

Red Oxide latex
Black latex
Inca Gold acrylic

Antique Gold acrylic
Silver Sterling acrylic
Pearl White acrylic

1 Using the base coat brush, prime the frame with white primer. Let dry, then sand and remove the sanding dust with a tack cloth. Base coat the frame in Red Oxide flat latex paint for the gold bee motif or in Black flat latex paint for the silver bee motif. (A flat-painted base coat will yield a better stencilled effect than a satin or semigloss base. The latter base paints will cause the stencilling to smear on the surface.)

STENCILLING: BEE MOTIF

2 Find the center point of the frame, then use a pencil and ruler to mark 1-inch (3cm) intervals out from the center on all sides of the frame. Ask an assistant to hold a chalk line string across the frame surface. Snap the string to create white lines across the frame. These will be your guidelines for placing the bee stencils. To make the stencils, use a fine-point marker to draw the pattern on a sheet of acetate. Place the acetate on a pane of glass and use a stencil-burning tool or craft knife to cut out the shapes.

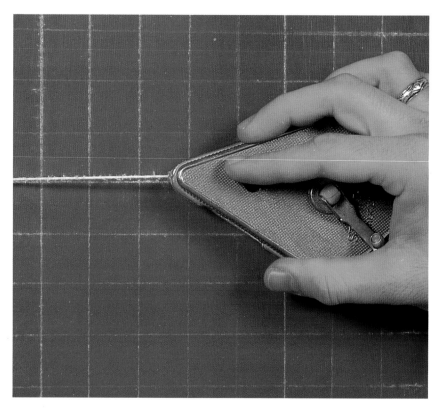

3 Place the stencil of the body of the bee on the cross point of every other crossline on the grid. Center the bee's body over the crosslines, and tape the stencil in position. Using a stencil brush loaded lightly with a dark metallic paint (here Antique Gold), stipple on the color. To stipple, simply pat the brush up and down depositing paint. Alternate the direction of the bees in each row across the frame.

4 Paint the wings of the bees using a lighter metallic shade. In this example, Inca Gold was stencilled on the wings. Place stencil on the frame using each bee's body as a guideline. Stipple on color.

5 Finish stencilling by painting in the details of the bees' heads and stripes. Carefully stipple the lighter metallic color, otherwise excessive pressure on the small openings in the stencil will smear these detail markings. Remove chalk lines by dusting the surface with a moist sponge. Add a fine stripe to the perimeter of the frame with a liner brush or ruling pen and thin-consistency metallic color.

PAPER COVERING: NATURAL

Photo of detail on natural paper covering.

here are so many beautiful handmade papers created from a diverse collection of natural materials. You can find papers embedded with flower petals, leaves, wild reeds, dried plant materials, rice and tree bark. These papers can become a subtle decorating element on a picture frame. Since the paper surface is already embellished with these embedded patterns, you do not need to elaborate or add decoration. This natural paper technique is perfect for framing items with natural themes—animal photos, dried and pressed flowers or botanical artwork. ❧

TOOLS AND MATERIALS

Natural papers

Brayer

Plastic tub

Sandpaper

Pencil

Tack cloth

Craft knife

Sponge brush

Base coat brush

White primer

Ruler

White eraser

Sponge

White glue

Not Shown
Plastic triangle with
45-degree angle

COLOR CHIPS—WATER-BASED PRIMER

White

1 Using the base coat brush, prime the picture frame with white primer. Sand the surface with fine-grade sandpaper, and remove any sanding dust with a tack cloth.

PAPER COVERING: NATURAL

2 Cut four strips of paper, one for each frame side. To determine how large to make your strips, measure the width and length of each side. Add an extra inch to the width to allow for wrapping the paper around the back of the frame. Mark the paper with a ruler and light pencil lines. Using a plastic triangle and a craft knife, cut the ends at 45-degree angles to create the mitered corners.

3 Using a sponge brush, coat the back of one piece of paper at a time with white glue that has been thinned down with water to a thin, creamy consistency. Immediately place the paper strip on the frame section.

4 Using a brayer, roll over the paper to squeeze out excess glue and remove air bubbles. The brayer will also ensure that the paper and glue have come in contact with the frame surface. Use the brayer to fold the excess paper around the back of the frame.

5 Remove extra glue from the paper with a clean kitchen sponge that has been lightly moistened with water. Repeat steps three and four for the remaining three sides of the frame. Be sure the mitered corners overlap slightly so no gaps show, and remove all excess glue. Let the paper dry thoroughly before erasing any visible pencil lines.

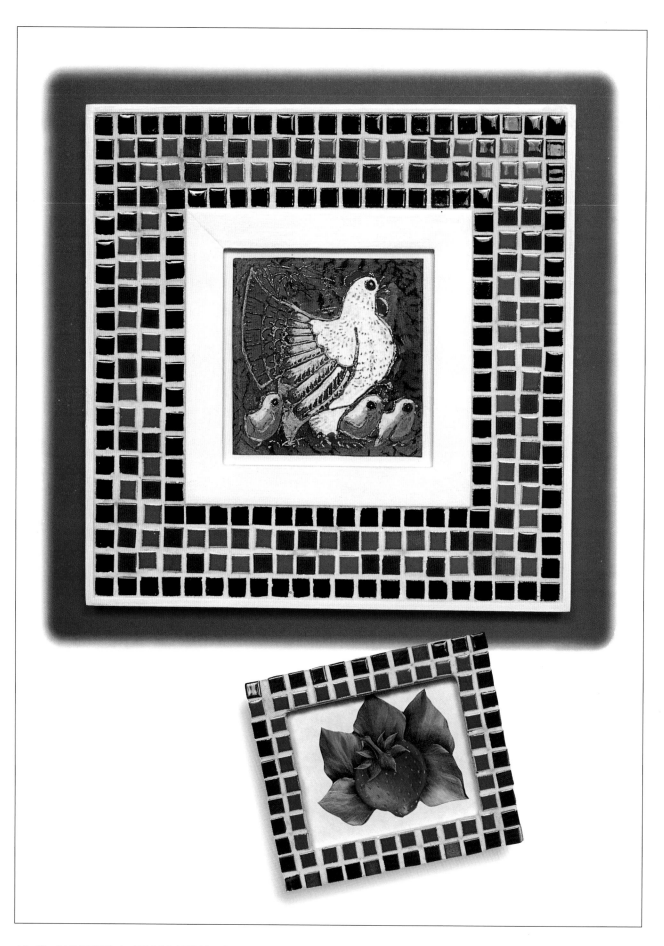

TILING: MOSAIC APPLICATION

Photo of detail on tile mosaic frame.

A mosaic is a decorative design made by setting small colored pieces, such as tiles or tesserae (small squares of glass), into a mortar or grout base. The addition of mosaic tiles to a picture frame adds a casual flair—a great look for kitchen, sunroom, greenhouse, deck or breakfast room settings.

You can place mosaics in a variety of patterns from simple graphic borders to specific imagery. For example, quilt patterns and Amish hex signs are ideal sources of inspiration when creating mosaic designs. ❧

TOOLS AND
MATERIALS

Mosaic adhesive

Plastic tub

Grout

Sandpaper

Mosaic tiles

Tack cloth

White primer

Paint stirrer

Base coat brush

Kitchen sponge

COLOR CHIPS—LATEX SEMIGLOSS PAINT

White

1 Using the base coat brush, prime the frame with white primer. Let dry. Sand the frame and remove any sanding dust with the tack cloth. Base coat the frame with White latex semigloss paint.

TILING: MOSAIC APPLICATION

2 Determine the basic placement of the mosaic tiles to create the pattern you have chosen. In this example, a simple linear border of colored tiles was used. Begin by placing the outer row of tiles around the perimeter of the frame. Work from both corners toward the center of each frame side. Place a small amount of tile adhesive on the back of each mosaic tile and press it onto the surface. You can adjust the tiles for a period of time to achieve the proper spacing.

3 Fill in the next two rows with alternating colors of tiles, adjusting the tiles as you go to achieve fairly even spacing. Again, work from both corners toward the center of each side to ensure a good lineup. Keep in mind that mosaic patterning and lineup is usually more casual than a tight kitchen tile grid.

4 Complete the final placement of the mosaic tile squares. Now is the time to make any last minute placement adjustments. If you do pick up a tile to adjust it, add a little more mosaic adhesive before positioning it in its new place.

5 To prepare the grout, mix the tile grout powder with adhesive or water following the manufacturer's label. Place the powder in a plastic tub, and mix with a paint stirrer until it reaches a consistency similar to thick oatmeal. Apply the grout between the tiles, forcing it into all crevices with your fingertips. Wipe away the excess grout with a moist kitchen sponge. Let dry. Using a clean, wet sponge, clean away grout haze and buildup on tiles.

STRIPING:
DRIED FLOWER APPLICATION

Photo of detail on striped frame with dried flower embellishment.

*P*ainted stripes are a popular decorating pattern. They create a striking background for just about anything you wish to place over them. In this example, dried roses, leaves, phylica and silk ribbon placed over the pink stripes establish a feminine theme. However, you could easily change the color scheme to a tan and cream stripe, place neutral-colored dried flowers and add a burlap ribbon for a country appearance. Or be creative with a montage of old coins, stamps, seashells and other memorabilia. Imagine how patriotic a photo of your family's war hero would look in a red-and-white-striped frame with medals of honor attached. ❧

TOOLS AND
MATERIALS

Phylica or baby's breath

Dried roses

Hot glue gun

*Hot glue
sticks*

Craft knife

Sandpaper

Ruler

Base coat brush

Tack cloth

*Burnishing
tool or spoon*

*White
primer*

*Wash
brush*

Pencil

Artist's white tape

*Silk ribbon,
wire edged*

COLOR CHIPS—LATEX SEMIGLOSS PAINT

Coral Pink

Light Pink

1 Using the base coat brush, prime the frame with white primer. Sand the frame with fine sandpaper. Remove any sanding dust with a tack cloth. Apply several coats of the Coral Pink or Light Pink latex paint with the base coat brush to achieve an opaque coverage.

2 To create crisp edges on the stripes, use artist's white tape as a mask. Locate the center point of the frame and place the first strip of tape so it is centered on that point. Next use the pencil and ruler to measure and mark light guidelines for placing the other tape strips. You can make the painted stripes the width of the tape for easy tape placement. In this example, ¾-inch (2cm) tape was used, so the painted stripes are made that wide.

3 Rub the tape's edges with the tip of a spoon or burnishing tool. This will prevent the paint from bleeding under the tape. Using a contrasting value of the base color, paint the stripes. Load a wash brush with color, and stroke on paint in a linear fashion. Let dry and apply a second coat.

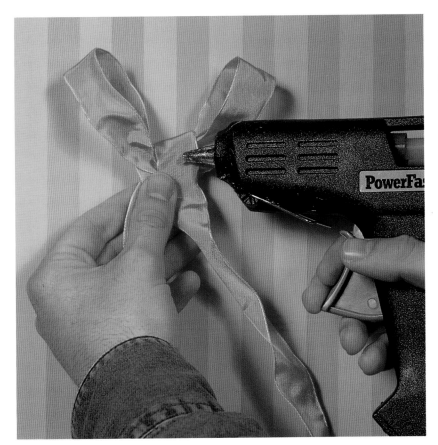

4 After the paint has dried thoroughly, remove the tape. Pull tape up slowly, always checking to see if any base coat or stripe color begins to pull up. If this occurs, run a craft knife along the tape edge to separate paint away from tape. Next cut the dried flowers and leaves into small, manageable units and cut a long length of ribbon for the bow and streamers. Tentatively determine the placement of the flowers, leaves and ribbon. Center the bow at the top and hot glue it in place.

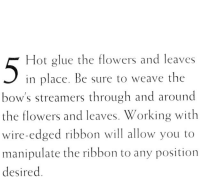

5 Hot glue the flowers and leaves in place. Be sure to weave the bow's streamers through and around the flowers and leaves. Working with wire-edged ribbon will allow you to manipulate the ribbon to any position desired.

STAMPING:
PEAR AND LEAF MOTIF

Photo of detail on pearl-stamped frame.

*S*tamping designs can be a fun and easy way to repeat a decorative pattern quickly on a frame surface. The choices in designs are endless, but a starting point often comes from reference materials. Designs to turn into stamps can be found in fabric, wallpaper and rugs in your home. When selecting a design to turn into a stamp, look for a simple shape that can be *read* (recognized) without a lot of detail. In these examples, pears and leaves have been stamped on the surfaces in a floating pattern.

TOOLS AND MATERIALS

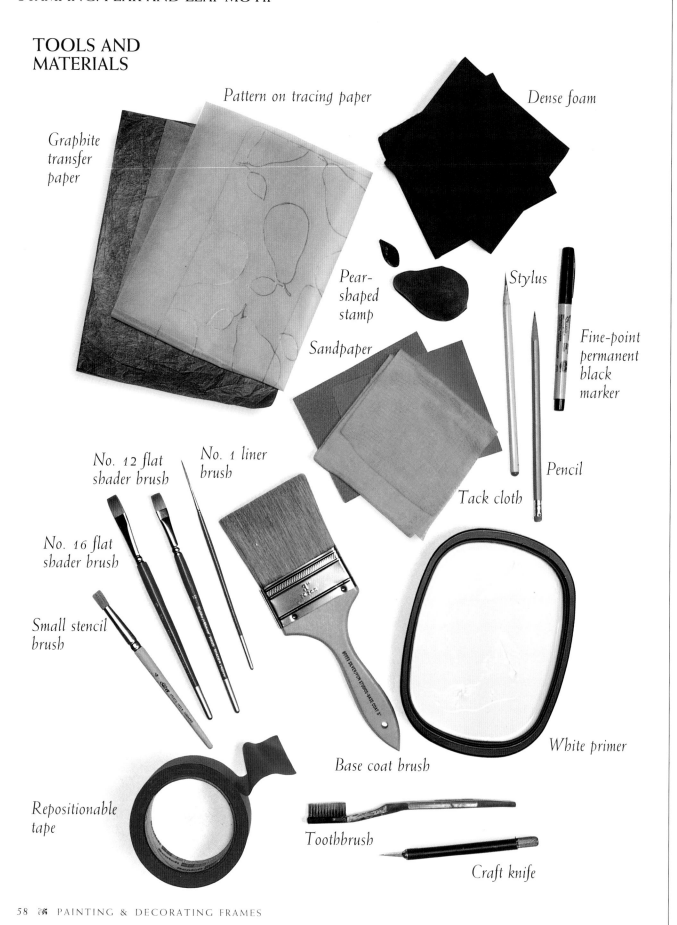

Pattern on tracing paper

Dense foam

Graphite transfer paper

Pear-shaped stamp

Stylus

Fine-point permanent black marker

Sandpaper

No. 12 flat shader brush

No. 1 liner brush

Tack cloth

Pencil

No. 16 flat shader brush

Small stencil brush

White primer

Base coat brush

Repositionable tape

Toothbrush

Craft knife

COLOR CHIPS—LATEX FLAT PAINT, ARTIST'S ACRYLICS

Cream latex
Yellow Ochre
Cadmium Yellow
 Light

Burnt Sienna
Phthalo Green
Ultramarine Blue

Titanium White
Ice Blue mix—
 Titanium White
 plus Phthalo
 Green plus
 Ultramarine Blue

1 Using the base coat brush, prime the frame with white primer. Let dry. Sand and remove any dust with a tack cloth. Using a base coat application brush, apply several smooth coats of cream flat latex paint. (A semigloss paint will not work for this technique.) Allow each coat to dry thoroughly before applying another coat. You want to achieve a pure, opaque cream coating.

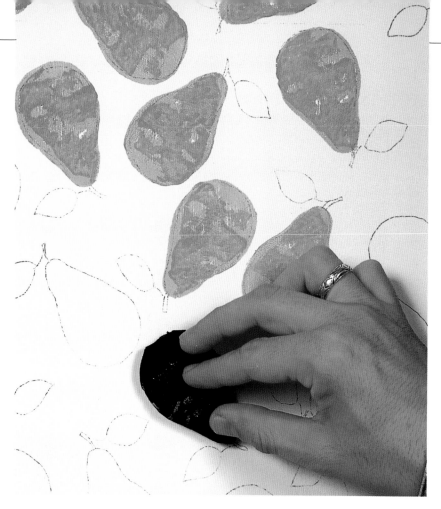

2 Using a craft knife, cut stamps out of dense foam by taping your pattern over the foam surface. You can choose to stamp the design free-form or plan the placement in advance. For advance placement, use a pencil and tracing paper to map out the design. Tape the design in place on the frame, and transfer it with graphite paper. Then load the pear stamp with Yellow Ochre using a no. 16 flat brush and press the stamp on the surface.

3 To create a shaded tone on the pear, load the same stamp with Yellow Ochre in the center and Burnt Sienna on the right outside edge and part of the bottom left outside edge. Stamp these tones over the yellow base. Try to apply the stamp in the same place. If it is not exact, that is all right. Let dry.

4 To soften the strong contrast on the pear, use the no. 16 flat brush to load the entire pear stamp with Cadmium Yellow Light. Press over each pear a third time. This will help the three colors blend.

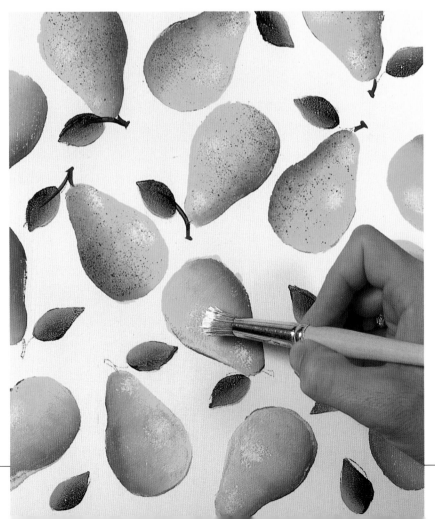

5 Highlight two loose oval shapes on the right side of the pears by using a small stencil brush to stipple on Titanium White. Create brown flecks on the pear by flyspecking the pear with thin-consistency Burnt Sienna. To flyspeck, load the toothbrush with paint and, pointing the toothbrush at the surface, run your thumb over the bristles. Stamp on leaves with Phthalo Green. Highlight the edges of the leaves with the Ice Blue mixture by stamping a second time. Paint the leaf stem with a liner brush and thin-consistency green, or the pear stem with brown.

PAPER COVERING: CORRUGATED

Photo of detail on corrugated paper covering.

*C*orrugated paper creates a wavy repetitive pattern that can be an attractive addition to any frame. The linear patterning of the paper makes it a perfect candidate to develop striped designs out of different colored papers. A natural-toned paper and a deep green-toned paper were used in these examples for a bold contrasting effect. Papers closer in value will create a softer more subtle effect. For framing a nature theme or masculine theme, choose corrugated papers in earth tones. ❧

TOOLS AND MATERIALS

Plastic tub

White craft glue

Kitchen sponge

Sandpaper

Pencil

Wash brush

Sponge brush

Tack cloth

Craft knife

Ruler

Base coat brush

White primer

Nail file or emery board

Corrugated cardboard

COLOR CHIPS—LATEX FLAT PAINT

Tan *Forest Green*

1 Using the base coat brush, prime the frame with white primer. Let dry. Sand and remove any sanding dust with a tack cloth. Base coat the frame with coordinating colors from the papers. In this example, Tan was placed on the flat surface and the sides of the frame were trimmed in Forest Green.

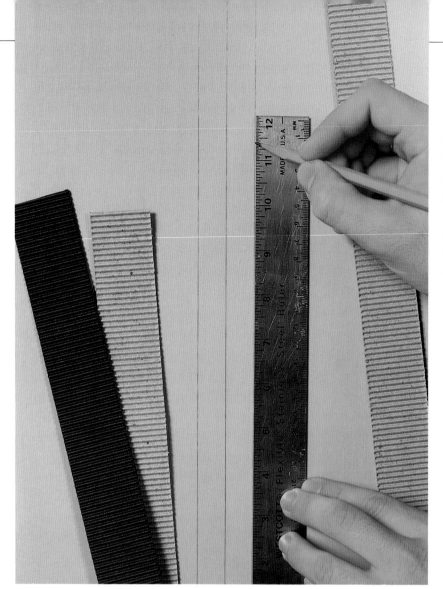

2 Determine the width of the strips of paper to be placed on the frame. Using a ruler and pencil, mark the back of the corrugated paper with that measurement. Cut the strips of paper using the ruler and a craft knife. Then measure and mark the center point on the frame. Center the first strip of corrugated paper at the frame's center point.

3 In a plastic tub, slightly thin the white glue with water until it reaches a thin, creamy consistency. Turn over the first strip of paper to be glued and use the sponge brush to coat it with glue. Immediately turn the paper over and put it in place. Press lightly with your fingertips.

4 Continue gluing the strips of corrugated paper side by side. Do your best to line up the corrugated grooves in the paper. If any excessive amounts of glue come out between the strips, wipe them lightly with a moist kitchen sponge. Be careful not to get the paper extremely wet or it could tear.

5 Finish placing the strips across the frame, and let them dry thoroughly. Then using the craft knife, trim any excess paper on the outside and inside edges, being careful not to scratch the painted surface. Use an emery board or nail file to smooth any corrugated cut edges.

GLUING: SEASHELL APPLICATION

Photo of detail on seashell frame.

A collection of seashells can bring back a wealth of memories of beautiful days at the ocean. Placing the shells on a frame allows you to combine nautical artwork or photographs with your collection. You can also add seaside driftwood, stones and rocks for a more rustic look. Or a similar effect could be achieved by collecting natural items found outdoors. If you love the water and nature, this is a great decorating approach, perfect for a home office, powder room or sunroom. 🍂

TOOLS AND MATERIALS

White glue

Gloss varnish

Kitchen sponge

Sandpaper

Tack cloth

Glaze/varnish brush

Base coat brush

White primer

Seashells

COLOR CHIPS—LATEX SEMIGLOSS PAINT, WATER-BASED GLAZE

Steel Gray latex   *Buttercream glaze*

1 Using the base coat brush, prime the frame with white primer and let dry. Sand with fine sandpaper, and remove the sanding dust with a tack cloth. Using the same brush, base coat the frame in several coats of Steel Gray semigloss latex paint until an opaque coverage is achieved. Allow the paint to thoroughly dry and cure before proceeding.

GLUING: SEASHELL APPLICATION

2 Lay out the collection of shells. If they are extremely dirty, wash them with soap and water and allow to dry. Experiment with the general placement of the shells and rocks on the picture frame. When satisfied with the arrangement, take one shell at a time, place a fair amount of white glue on the back of it and press in place.

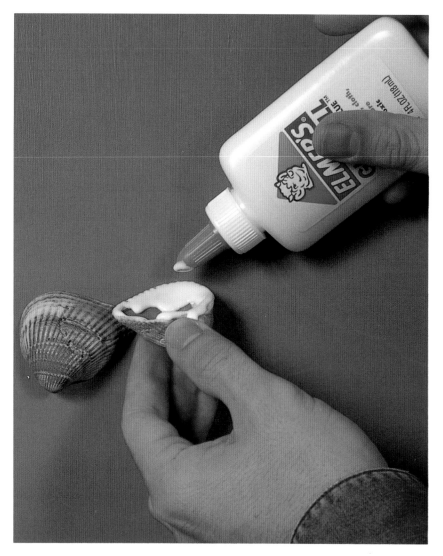

3 Continue to layer more shells and rocks on the frame until you have achieved a pleasing overall placement. Before glue sets, make any last-minute adjustments. Let glue and shells dry overnight before proceeding.

4 To create a little paint texture on the frame and pull the seashells' coloring together, glaze the entire surface. Using a cream-toned glaze and a glaze application brush, stipple color over the entire frame and shells. Bounce the brush up and down on the surface to form air bubbles that will resemble ocean foam. Let dry.

5 To bring the glaze coloring up and show off the shells, stipple on two coats of a gloss water-based varnish. This will also help disguise any glossiness from the dried glue that may be showing around the seashells.

ANTIQUING: GAME BOARD MOTIF

Photo of detail on game board motif frame.

*O*ld game boards have become quite a collector's item. You can mimic the feeling of these old game boards on picture frames by borrowing some of their bold, graphic patterns. To further imitate an old-fashioned look, use distressing and antiquing techniques to add to the authenticity you are trying to achieve. The finished look will be a warm, country decorating style suitable for casual rooms in the home—a family room, den or country-style kitchen. ❧

TOOLS AND MATERIALS

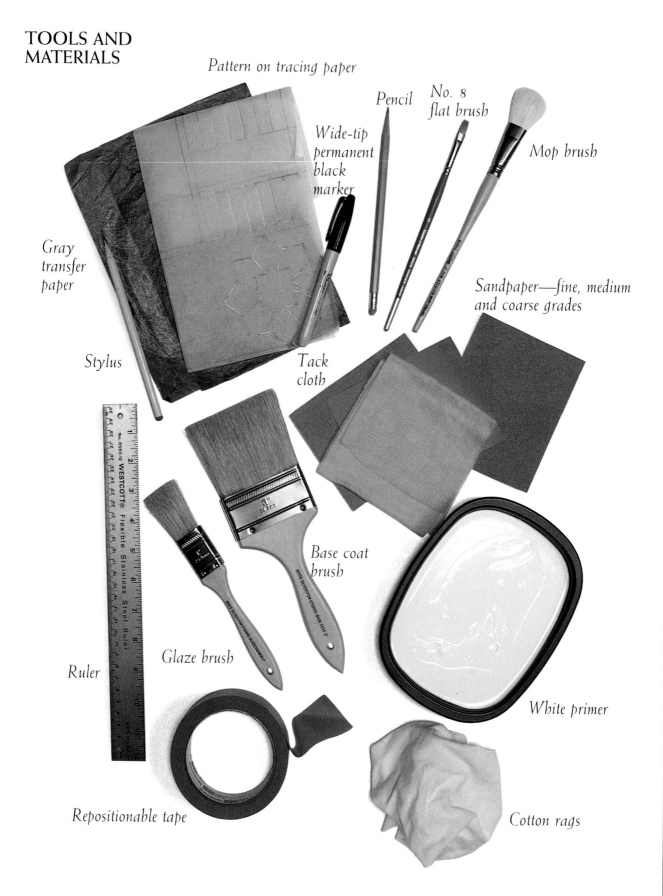

Pattern on tracing paper

Pencil

No. 8
flat brush

Wide-tip
permanent
black
marker

Mop brush

Gray
transfer
paper

Sandpaper—fine, medium
and coarse grades

Stylus

Tack
cloth

Ruler

Glaze brush

Base coat
brush

White primer

Repositionable tape

Cotton rags

COLOR CHIPS—LATEX FLAT PAINT, WATER-BASED GLAZE

White latex
Opaque Red latex
Dark Blue latex

Dark Brown glaze

1 Using the base coat brush, prime the frame with white primer. Let dry. Sand the frame with fine sandpaper, and remove the sanding dust with a tack cloth. Base coat the frame in several coats of White flat latex. Using flat paint will ensure smooth sanding in the distressing steps.

2 Transfer the graphic design to the frame surface by taping the tracing paper pattern to the frame and slipping the transfer paper underneath. Go over the lines with a ruler and stylus. Using a no. 8 flat brush, begin filling in sections of the design. Here, Opaque Red is used in the background and in some of the stripes.

3 Next, using the flat brush, apply the blue to the stripes and arrow-point shapes. Apply several coats until a fairly opaque coverage is achieved. Since you will be distressing the paint, a total opaque coverage is not necessary.

4 To define sections of the outside edges, go over the perimeter of all of the shapes with a ruler and wide-tip permanent black marker. Then using a medium- or coarse-grade sandpaper, sand over the design to distress the surface. This step can be done as lightly or heavily as you desire.

5 To antique the game board frame, brush on Dark Brown glaze across the surface using a glaze application brush. Use a clean cotton rag to wipe off the excess glaze in a linear direction. Just like distressing, you can antique the surface as lightly or as heavily as you desire. Use the mop brush to softly blend the antiquing.

TILING: BROKEN CHINA

Photo of detail on broken china frame.

*H*ere's a simple tiling technique that can take the accident of a broken china plate, teacup or bowl and turn it into a decorating tool. Whether you use this accident to your advantage or break some china deliberately, you can decorate a frame with broken china to create a casual appearance suitable for the kitchen or breakfast room. You can also mix broken china with other broken elements (tile and glass) or other small found objects (coins and keys). ❧

TOOLS AND MATERIALS

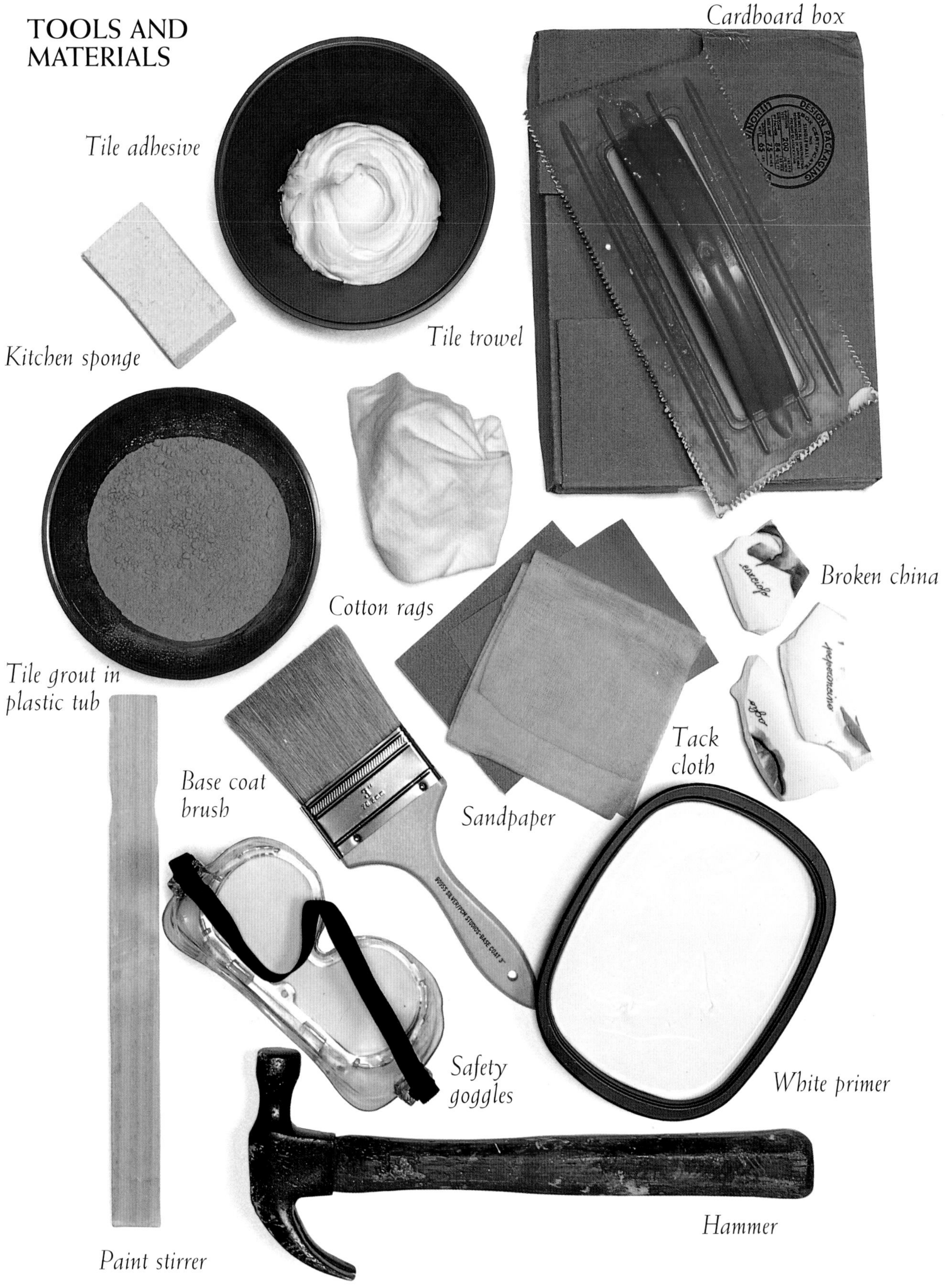

Tile adhesive

Kitchen sponge

Tile trowel

Cardboard box

Cotton rags

Broken china

Tile grout in plastic tub

Base coat brush

Sandpaper

Tack cloth

Safety goggles

White primer

Paint stirrer

Hammer

COLOR CHIPS—LATEX FLAT PAINT

Gray Green

1 Using the base coat brush, prime frame with white primer. Let dry. Sand and remove any sanding dust with a tack cloth. If you plan on covering the entire frame in tile grout, no base coat is necessary. But if the frame edges or trim will show, base coat the frame in a coordinating color with a flat latex paint.

2 To break the china, put on the safety goggles, place the china in a cardboard box, pick up the hammer and place your hand, while holding the hammer, inside the box. Loosely close the flaps of the box. Strike the china piece with the hammer at a central point. Open the flaps and determine if additional hits are needed to break the china into manageable pieces for the picture frame's size.

3 To prepare the frame, use the trowel to apply an even coating of tile adhesive on the surface. Stroke the surface several times with the trowel to create a fine network of grooves. Be sure the thickness of the adhesive coating is consistent so you can place the broken china evenly.

4 Begin placing the broken china pieces approximately ⅜ inch (1cm) apart around the perimeter of the frame. Press the china pieces into the adhesive to ensure good contact. Save the small pieces to use as fillers in the larger gaps. After all of the china pieces are in place, let the adhesive dry twenty-four hours.

5 Use the paint stirrer to mix the tile grout and water in a plastic tub according to the directions on the grout box. Begin working the grout into the spaces between the china pieces; use your hands, the tile trowel or the paint stirrer. Using a moist cotton rag, remove the excess grout and allow it to set up for about fifteen minutes.

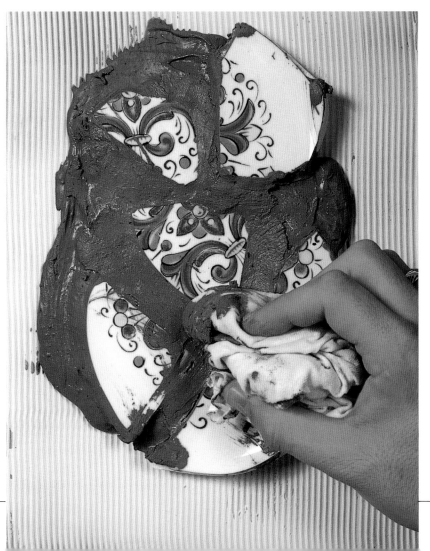

6 Moisten a cotton rag with water and wipe away the rest of the excess grout. Then let the grout dry until a haze forms over the china pieces (about forty minutes). Use a clean kitchen sponge moistened with water to clean off the grout haze.

Paper Covering: Script Parchment

Photo of detail on parchment-covered frame.

*E*laborate handwritten script and famous quotes have popped up on many surfaces these days, from furniture to accessories to walls. Here script parchment paper has covered the surface of the frame. Metallic Gold paint and gold leaf highlight the script writings. You can create your own script paper or use a ready-made paper. If you want to personalize your script, handmade paper is the technique for you. If you desire a more exact look, use a manufactured paper.

TOOLS AND MATERIALS

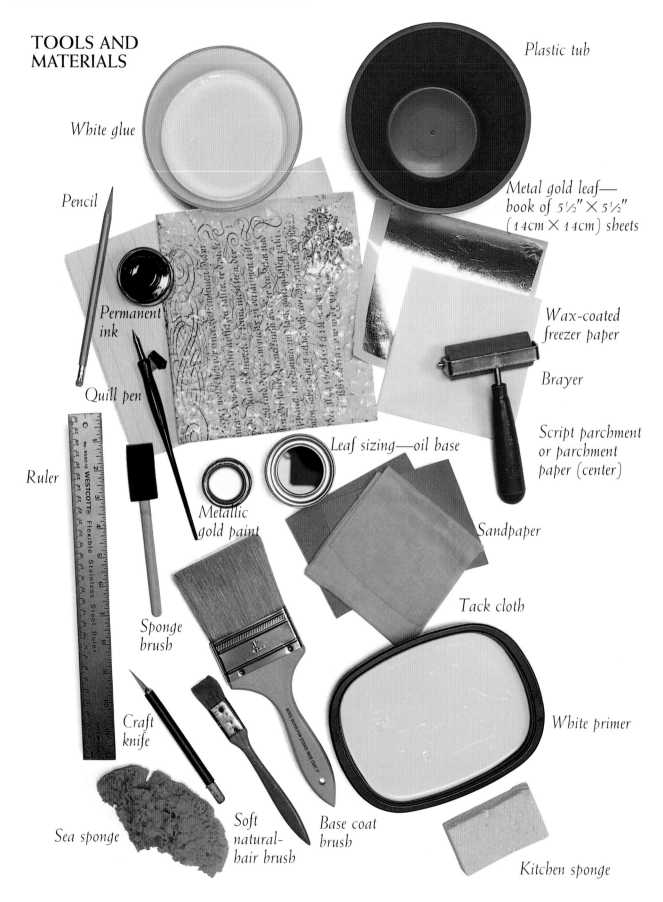

Plastic tub

White glue

Pencil

Metal gold leaf—
book of 5½" × 5½"
(14cm × 14cm) sheets

Permanent
ink

Wax-coated
freezer paper

Quill pen

Brayer

Leaf sizing—oil base

Script parchment
or parchment
paper (center)

Ruler

Metallic
gold paint

Sandpaper

Tack cloth

Sponge
brush

White primer

Craft
knife

Sea sponge

Soft
natural-
hair brush

Base coat
brush

Kitchen sponge

COLOR CHIPS—LATEX SEMIGLOSS PAINT

White   *Metallic Gold*

1 Using the base coat brush, prime the frame with white primer. Let dry, then sand. Remove the sanding dust with a tack cloth. If you plan to cover the frame edges with gold leaf or gold paint, a base coat color is not necessary.

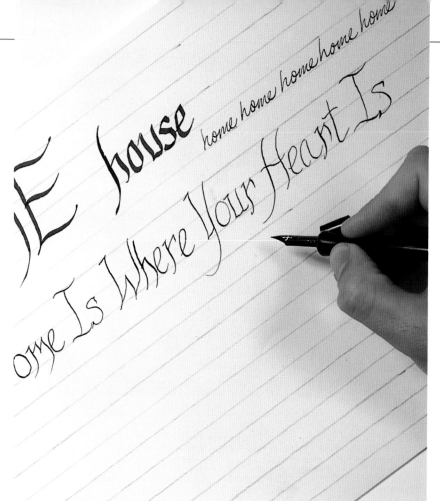

2 To create your own script parchment paper, practice a fluid writing style on scrap paper using a writing quill pen and permanent drawing ink. You can write freehand on the paper or create writing guidelines with light pencil marks and a ruler. Complete your script.

3 For added interest, crumple the paper loosely and smooth it out. Highlight the crumpled paper by loading a sponge brush with Metallic Gold paint and lightly dusting over the high spots. Let paper dry.

4 Cut the paper slightly larger (about 1 inch [3cm] on each side) than the surface to be covered. Using the sponge brush, brush white glue that has been thinned slightly with water onto the back of the paper. Lay the paper over the frame, and smooth it out by running a brayer across the surface to squeeze out excess glue and water. Clean up the glue with a moistened kitchen sponge. Let dry. Trim the extra paper off the edges using a sharp craft knife. Finish the edges of the frame with Metallic Gold paint or gold leaf.

Vinegar Painting: Texture Patterns

Photo of detail on vinegar-painted frame.

inegar painting was a favorite pastime in the Colonial period when decorating small objects and furniture—even frames—was completed by itinerant artisans. This technique yields a loose and abstract style of patterning. Fortunately, the medium is pretty forgiving, so you can play with the paint until you are pleased with the finished pattern. The patterned designs you can create are limitless—they are only bound by your creativity and imagination. ⁊

TOOLS AND MATERIALS

Oil-based polyurethane varnish

Sugar in mixing bowl

Spoon

Vinegar in measuring cup

Modeling clay

Sandpaper

Powdered pigments

Glaze/varnish brush

Tack cloth

Wash brush

White primer

Base coat brush

COLOR CHIPS—LATEX SEMIGLOSS PAINT, POWDERED PIGMENT

Tan latex
Burnt Umber powder
Burnt Sienna powder

1 Using the base coat brush, prime the frame with white primer. Let dry. Sand with fine sandpaper, and remove the sanding dust with a tack cloth. Apply several coats of Tan latex semigloss base coat until an opaque coverage is achieved.

VINEGAR PAINTING: TEXTURE PATTERNS

2 In a bowl, mix one teaspoon (5ml) of sugar into one cup (236ml) of vinegar. Slowly add one-half cup (118ml) of the powdered pigment to this mixture so that the vinegar to powdered pigment ratio is two to one. Experiment with this mixture by brushing it onto a scrap surface. If the vinegar paint beads up, add more powdered pigment to the mixture. Paint the surface with vinegar paint using a glaze brush. Apply an even coating in long, continuous strokes from one end of the frame to the other.

3 To texturize the paint, you can use just about any item for making marks—modeling clay, corncobs, fingers. Be creative. Here a cylinder of modeling clay was rolled across the wet paint in a linear fashion.

4 Roll the cylinder of clay with your fingertips, moving diagonally to further embellish the pattern. This will break up the vertical pattern completed in the last step. Let dry.

5 Seal the frame with an oil-based varnish. (A water-based varnish will cause the paint pattern to run and smear.) Apply a smooth, even coat of varnish with a natural-bristle brush.

GLUING: BUTTON APPLICATION

Photo of detail on button-applied frame.

utton collecting and button crafting have become popular in recent years, so it seems logical to decorate frames with buttons, too. Other elements can be added to the buttons, such as jewelry, beads or watch parts. Sewing elements could also be added, including thimbles, needles and thread bobbins. Adding buttons to a frame is a quick and easy project and one that children could create successfully. Frames decorated in this motif are ideal gifts for a seamstress, tailor or quilter. ✄

GLUING: BUTTON APPLICATION

TOOLS AND MATERIALS

White glue

Buttons

Sandpaper

Jewelry embellishments

Tack cloth

Base coat brush

Varnish brush

White primer

Not Shown
Water-based gloss varnish

COLOR CHIPS—LATEX SEMIGLOSS PAINT

Bright Red

1 Using the base coat brush, prime the frame with white primer. Let dry. Sand the frame with fine sandpaper, and remove the sanding dust with a tack cloth. Base coat the frame in a coordinating color to go with the buttons. Apply several coats until opaque coverage is achieved.

GLUING: BUTTON APPLICATION

2 Experiment with the button placement to determine the overall patterning. Here a background layer of different sizes of red buttons was placed on the surface. To attach the buttons, apply a liberal amount of glue on the back of each button and press in the desired location.

3 Continue to lay in the background buttons until the surface is covered. Adjust any final placement of the buttons at this time before allowing the glue to dry for six to eight hours. Giving the glue this drying time before layering on more buttons or jewelry will cause less shifting of the top layer of items.

4 Add a second layer of elements. Glue the buttons or other items in place using a liberal amount of glue on the back of each item and pressing firmly. Let these new items dry overnight.

5 To eliminate the visible glossiness of the dried glue, brush on a coat or two of gloss water-based varnish. Lightly brush the surface of the buttons and frame with varnish using a varnish application brush. Be careful not to apply too much varnish.

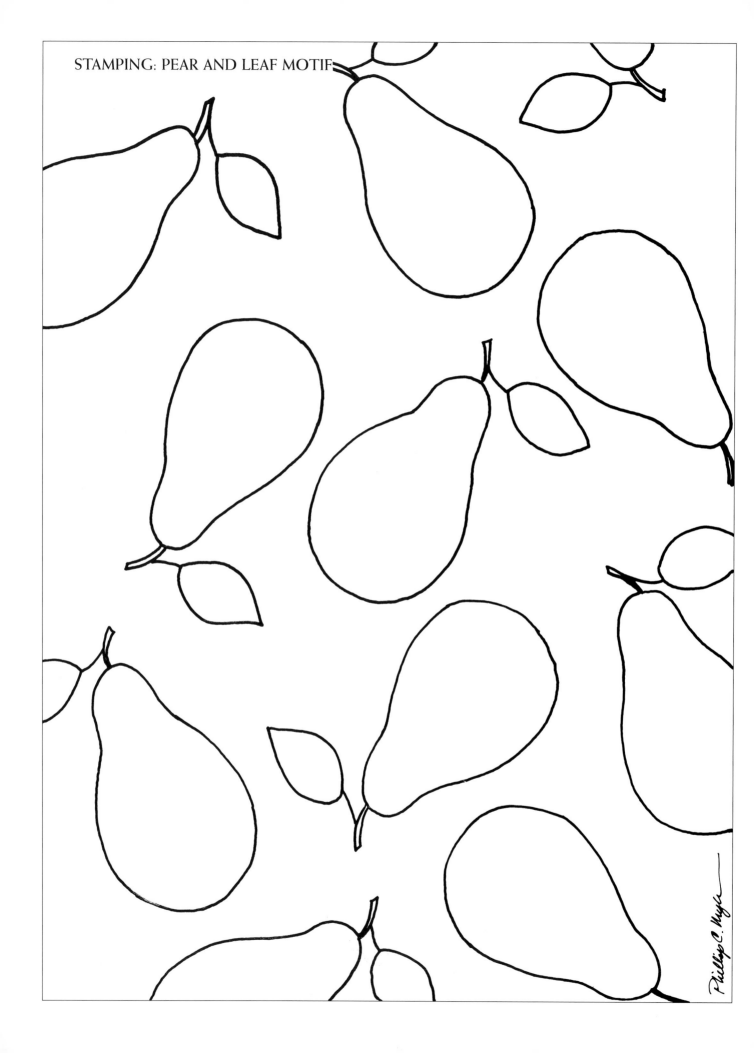

STAMPING: PEAR AND LEAF MOTIF

Phillip C. Myer

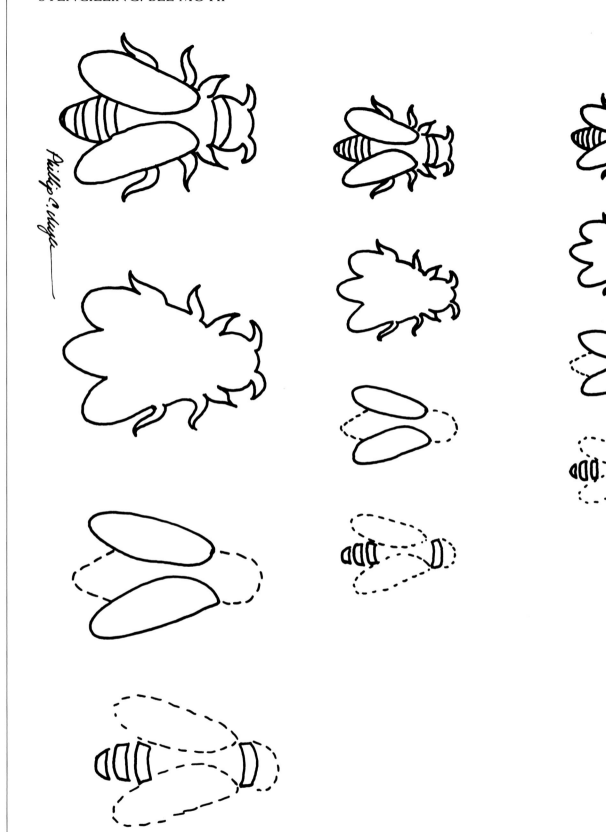

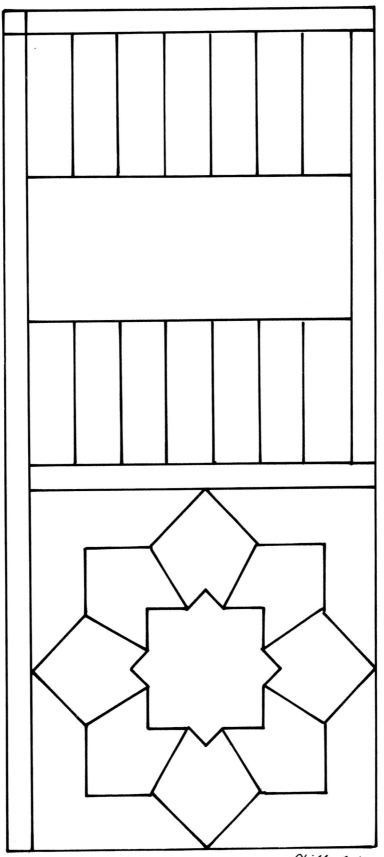

GLOSSARY

ACRYLIC POLYMER—a thermoplastic resin with a synthetic substance or mixture used as a binder with powdered pigments in the creation of artist's acrylic colors.

ANTIQUING—the application of a very thin, transparent coating over a surface to give the illusion of age and patina.

ARTIST'S ACRYLIC COLORS—paint that is a mixture of powdered pigments ground in thermoplastic, synthetic emulsions, which can be thinned and cleaned up with water.

BASE COAT—the initial application of paint to a surface.

BODY—the weight or form of an object or substance; as it relates to paint, the consistency or thickness.

BRAYER—a small tool made with a rubber roller and metal or wooden handle, used as a hand roller for applying pressure.

BURNISH—to polish or rub a surface with a hard tool to adhere and smooth areas.

CHEESECLOTH—a coarse woven fabric made from cotton gauze.

CHISEL—the sharp edge on the bristle end of a well-crafted flat brush.

COLOR VALUES—the degrees of lightness, darkness, saturation and brightness of a hue.

CORRUGATED—a surface, usually paper, that has been pressed to form parallel, alternating ridges and grooves.

CRACKLED—random separations in a paint or varnish finish that make the object appear older than it really is; can result from product incompatibility, temperature or weather.

CRISSCROSS—a paint stroke direction that forms randomly crossed lines.

CURTAINING—the sagging or dripping of a layer of paint or varnish that has been placed over a previous coat that is not cured and dried; the top layer weights down the first layer that is not dried and pulls both layers down like a sagging curtain.

DARK VALUE—the deeper color tones that can be created by mixing any color with black or its color complement.

DECORATIVE PAINTING—an ornamental art form used to decorate functional as well as nonfunctional surfaces; it is a teachable art form broken down into step-by-step methods.

DECOUPAGE—the French art form of cutting and pasting images to form decorative treatments on a surface.

DISTRESSING—the action of battering a surface through the use of abrasive tools, such as sandpaper, hammers, nails, screws or chains; the goal is to imitate the wear and tear of an aged surface.

EARTH TONES—colors that are made with natural pigments, such as Yellow Ochre, which is made from refined clay.

FAUX—the French word that translates as false or fake; as it relates to paint, a look that mimics a real surface, for example, faux marble—painted to look like marble; faux bois—painted to look like wood grain.

FLAT—as it relates to paint, the sheen or finish that is dull and porous.

FLECKS—small particles of paint spattered on a surface.

FLYSPECKING—the painting technique that disperses small particles of paint over the surface with the use of a toothbrush and thin-consistency paint.

FOIL GILDING—an inexpensive and quick technique using foil to simulate the look of traditional, metal leaf gilding.

FREEHAND—to create without the use of patterns or guidelines.

FREEZER PAPER—a paper that has a plastic coating on one side and is used to wrap foods for storage in the freezer.

GILDING—the process of applying gold, silver or other metal leaf to a surface.

GLAZE—a transparent mixture of color plus a clear painting medium.

GLOSS—the highest level of a finish's sheen or shine qualities.

GRAY SCALE—a standardized, incremental chart of values from white to black (light to dark).

GRID—a framed structure of equally spaced parallel and perpendicular lines used to paint various tile or stripe patterns; also used to enlarge or reduce the size of designs by scaling them up or down proportionately.

HAZE—a transparent but cloudy or smoky coating over a surface that obstructs the clarity of the color below.

HIGH CONTRAST—an extreme value difference in close proximity; the highest level would be from white to gray to black in a short distance.

HUE—the qualities of color; the intensity of color, as in a shade or tint.

INKLIKE CONSISTENCY—paint thinned with painting medium, painting glaze or solvent to the liquid state that matches drawing ink.

ITINERANT ARTISAN—a creative individual who travels from place to place to perform artistic tasks or jobs.

LATEX—paint made from powdered pigment ground with emulsion of rubber or plastic globules; can be cleaned with water.

LIFTOFF—the intentional or accidental removal of a base coat, paint finish or varnish.

LIGHT VALUE—the brighter color values on the gray scale; any color can become a lighter value through the addition of white.

MARBLEIZED PAPER—a fiber surface that has been decorated with pigments and solutions to create wavy, swirling patterns.

MARBLEIZING—the act of reproducing a marble pattern through the use of paint applied with a brush and/or feathers on a surface.

MASKING—to mark off an area and then protect it by covering with tape or other items so it won't receive paint when a nearby area is being painted.

MEDIUM—the type of paint used, such as acrylics or oils; or a liquid, such as water-based varnish, acrylic retarder or water, used to thin acrylic paints.

MEDIUM VALUE—a color tone in the middle of the value range between light and dark.

METALLIC—a surface or paint that has the characteristics and qualities of a metal.

MIDTONE—the center point of a color's value in relation to its lightest or darkest points within a given painted area.

MONTAGE—to overlap design elements on a surface until very little or none of the original surface shows; a technique employed in decoupage.

MOSAIC—a design or picture made from placing small colored pieces (usually tile) in adhesive, then surrounding the pieces with grout or mortar.

MULTITONE—the development of a variety of values of one color or many colors on a surface.

NATURAL PAPERS—sheets of material made from processed pulp of wood, fabric and certain grasses, with other items such as flower petals, leaves and reeds embedded into the surface.

OPAQUE—paint coverage so thick that light cannot pass through it.

OPEN TIME—the period in which the paints, painting mediums or varnishes will remain workable before they begin to set up and dry.

PAINT RUNS—usually undesirable drips of paint or varnish that move down a vertical surface.

PASTE WAX—a coating of semisolid wax, rubbed on and buffed off to add a level of polish and sheen to a surface.

PATINA—the characteristic marks and signs of age that develop on a surface; the corrosion that occurs as metals oxidize.

PATTERN—a guideline to follow when creating, as in woodworking, sewing or decorative painting.

POROUS—a surface that has permeable openings that moisture easily penetrates.

PRIMER—an opaque, paintlike base coat application that seals the surface and readies it for decorative treatment; a stain-blocking sealer that prevents bottom coats from penetrating through.

QUILL PEN—a writing instrument made from a stemlike shaft of a feather or from metal shaped to resemble the feather's tip.

RETARDER—agents that suspend and slow down the quick drying time of some water-based products, such as acrylics.

RULING—the painted trim work of fine lines created through the application of thin-consistency paint with a ruling pen.

SAGGING—the lifting and dropping of a coat of paint due to improper surface preparation.

SATIN—a surface with a slight amount of sheen or shine; a step up from a flat finish.

SCRIPT—handwriting with cursive characters as distinguished from printing.

SEMIGLOSS—a surface with sheen level greater than satin but less than gloss.

SETUP TIME—the period it takes for paint, painting glazes or varnishes to begin to dry and become tacky.

SIDE LOAD—to carry color only on one side of the brush with painting medium or solvent on the other; to create a blended transition on the brush from opaque color to transparent color to no color.

SIZING—an adhesive used in the gilding process, brushed on to attach metal leaf to a surface.

SKEWINGS—small torn sections of metal leaf remaining after burnishing a gilded surface.

SOLVENT—the agent that cleans and thins paint, varnishes and painting mediums and can also be used as a painting medium; for example, the solvent for acrylic is water, the solvent for oils is turpentine.

SPACKLING COMPOUND—also called plaster patch, a thick-bodied, plasterlike substance used to fill holes.

SPONGING—the application of paint with a loaded sponge to create a textural pattern on a surface.

STAMPING—imprinting a surface with a design or pattern using a rubber or foam cutout.

STENCIL—a sheet of Mylar, acetate or heavy card stock with a design cut into it.

STENCILLING—the application of design work by brushing or spraying paint through a cut design opening.

STREAMER—a long narrow strip of material, such as ribbon.

STRIÉ—the painted finish technique that uses a flogger brush to create irregular linear streaks in a wet paint glaze.

STRIPING—the addition of horizontal or vertical lines (or a combination of both) in any degree of line width.

STRIPPING—the removal of paint, varnish or other buildup on a surface through the use of commercially made chemical products and scraping tools.

TACKY—a sticky quality that develops during the drying time of a paint product; some techniques require waiting for a tacky paint/glue/varnish state before proceeding with the technique.

TELEGRAPHING—the action of an impression or pattern coming up from a foundation level and exposing itself in the top layers of a surface coating.

TESSERA—a small square of glass or stone used in making mosaic patterns.

THICK, CREAMY CONSISTENCY—a paint mixed with a very small amount of painting medium, paint glaze or solvent and whipped to the texture of whipped butter so the paint holds peaks when patted with a palette knife.

THIN, CREAMY CONSISTENCY—a paint mixed with painting medium, paint glaze or solvent to the texture of whipped cream.

THIN, SOUPY CONSISTENCY—a paint mixed with painting medium, paint glaze or solvent to the texture of watered-down soup.

TONAL GRADATION—the creation of various color tones that intermingle and go down the gray scale in an even transition.

TONE ON TONE—the layering of two or more colors that are similar in lightness or darkness.

TRANSPARENT—a coating of paint or glaze so thin that light can easily pass through it.

VALUE—the ratio or percentage of color that relates to the gray scale; the variations of a color from lightest to darkest.

VARNISH—a clear coating of either a polyurethane-, water- or oil-based product that protects the coated surface.

VEINS—the interior structural pattern element found in leaf structures as well as marble surfaces.

WALLPAPER—a paper surface printed with colored patterns that is applied to walls as a decorative treatment.

WASH—paint that is thinned with enough painting medium, paint glaze or solvent to make it fluid and transparent.

WET SANDING—the smoothing of a surface with a fine, wet/dry sandpaper that is wet with water and soap; used in the finishing stage to remove any imperfections between coats of varnish.

WOOD GRAIN—the pattern of marks found in wood surfaces; a flowing organic pattern.

WOOD GRAINING—the painted finish that duplicates a wood type, achieved through the use of a wet paint glaze, brushes and tools.

WOOD PUTTY—the thick compound made of whiting, linseed oil and binders in a doughlike consistency, used to fill imperfections on a wood surface before painting or finishing.

SOURCES

The following companies are manufacturers, mail-order suppliers or facilities that offer the specific materials used in the creation of the decorated frames in this book. Please write for further information. Include a self-addressed, stamped return envelope to ensure a response.

BRUSHES (GOLDEN NATURAL AND FAUX FINISH BRUSHES)
Silver Brush Limited
92 N. Main St., Bldg. 18C
Windsor, NJ 08561
Phone: (609) 443-4900
Fax: (609) 443-4888

GLAZES, GLUES AND VARNISHES (ANITA'S FAUX EASY PRODUCTS)
Back Street, Inc.
3905 Steve Reynolds Blvd.
Norcross, GA 30093
Phone: (770) 381-7373
Fax: (770) 381-6424

PAINTS (PRIMA ARTIST'S ACRYLICS)
Martin/F. Weber Co.
2727 Southampton Rd.
Philadelphia, PA 19154
Phone: (215) 677-5600
Fax: (215) 677-3336

TAPES (SAFE RELEASE AND LONG-MASK TAPES)
3M Consumer Products Group
P.O. Box 33053
St. Paul, MN 55133
Phone: (612) 733-1110

UNFINISHED FRAMES
The following companies produce the unfinished frames decorated in this book. The decorated frames are referenced by techniques found in this book.

Hy-Jo MFG Imports Corp.
1830 John Towers Ave.
El Cajon, CA 92020
Phone: (800) 788-9969
Fax: (619) 449-8685
- Paper Covering—Marbleized
- Texturizing—Cheesecloth
- Paper Covering—Natural
- Tiling—Mosaic Application
- Gluing—Seashell Application
- Tiling—Broken China
- Vinegar Painting—Texture Patterns
- Gluing—Button Application

House Works, Ltd.
2388 Pleasantdale Rd.
Atlanta, GA 30340
Phone: (770) 448-6596
Fax: (770) 448-3350
- Gilding—Distressed

Walnut Hollow
Route 1
Dodgeville, WI 53533
Phone: (800) 950-5101
Fax: (608) 935-3029

- Stencilling—Bee Motif
- Striping—Dried Flower Application
- Stamping—Pear and Leaf Motif
- Paper Covering—Corrugated
- Antiquing—Game Board Motif
- Paper Covering—Script Parchment

SCHOOLS

The following are schools that specialize in the teaching of paint and faux finishes for the decoration of accessories, furniture and interiors.

American Academy of Decorative Finishes

14255 N. Seventy-ninth St., Suite 10
Scottsdale, AZ 85260
Phone: (602) 991-8560
Fax: (602) 991-9779

Day Studio Workshop, Inc.

1504 Bryant St.
San Francisco, CA 94103
Phone: (415) 626-9300

Finishing School, Inc.

334 Main St.
Port Washington, NY 11050
Phone: (516) 767-6422
Fax: (516) 767-7406

PCM Studios

School of the Decorative Arts
731 Highland Ave. NE, Suite D
Atlanta, GA 30312
Phone: (404) 222-0348
Fax: (404) 222-0348
E-mail: abjpcm@aol.com

Students at PCM Studios learning paint faux finishes.

INDEX